BECOMING A RESPONSIBLE STUDENT

by Alana L. Rister

All Rights Reserved.

Alana L. Rister is the exclusive owner of the manuscript. ©2019

No part of this publication can be reproduced, stored in a retrieval system, or transmitted in any form or by any means electronic, mechanical, photocopying, recording or otherwise without the written permission of the owner.

Published in the United States of America.

ISBN 978-1-951070-08-3

CONTENTS

Title Page
Introduction 1
The Illusion of the Perfect Student 5
Turning Assignments into Opportunities 12
Knowing What You Need To Do 20
Navigating Each Course to Success 28
Managing the Frustration 37
Reaching Out, But Not Too Much 42
Conclusion 49

INTRODUCTION

Becoming a responsible student may mean different things to different people. To some, being a responsible student may sound incredibly simple; yet, to others, it may sound confusing and overwhelming. However, a responsible student is not the same as a good or perfect student.

In fact, a good student has no definable or measurable qualities that apply to everyone. Is a good student someone who maintains a certain grade point average, has perfect attendance, or has the answer to every question? Depending on who you are and your values, your answer could be any one of these or something completely different all together. When attempting to succeed in school, it is important to become the best version of yourself, not just what a good student means to you.

"The outcome doesn't matter as long as you try your best." We have probably all heard these words. They are partly true in that your focus should be on doing your best instead of reaching for impossible goals. However, I think this is a difficult phrase to measure in actions and results because how do you truly know what your best is? How do you know if you are lacking the skills or perspective to be the best you can be? Based on this idea, I wrote this book about my own experience as a student and dealing with my fellow classmates and their struggles.

My academic career began in high school where I went to a public boarding school. During high school, I was fully responsible for my own education. There was no one telling me when or how to get work done. I was successful in obtaining a distinction in chemistry and foreign languages with a 3.99 GPA. I even worked as a chemistry and math tutor to my peers during this time. I had to develop skills that would allow me to be successful in school while dealing with many different courses.

While working as a tutor, I was privy to other students' problems and was in a position where I could help them to understand the course material to pass their tests and complete the work. However, I found that many times what they really needed was better time management and help identifying what was truly required to be successful in their studies. Many students do not have the necessary skills to truly become their best and reach their goals.

After high school, I went to Mary Baldwin College and was part of the corps of cadets. Initially, I started as a chemistry major but quickly added a minor in psychology and leadership studies. My sophomore year of college was a major turning point for me as a student. In the first half of my sophomore year, my first class of the day started at noon, so you would think that I would have had excellent attendance in that class. Unfortunately, I needed to mature more. I missed about a third of that class; amazingly, I even missed some days from oversleeping!

Starting in the second semester, several changes occurred in my personal and academic life. I had a major fight with my closest friend which caused serious difficulties in my social life which included alienation and rejection from others. Due to my habits the previous semester, I had received grades that I was not happy about but knew I completely deserved.

So, I decided to be a much more responsible student and rarely missed a class after that semester. I began to achieve better grades with less effort and allowed myself more flexibility in my academic future.

Due to these changes, I added a second major in sexuality and gender studies and a third minor in physics! I was able to graduate with a 3.93 GPA with two majors and three minors and several honors. My success was due to the changes I made in my sophomore year. The lessons I learned that sparked those changes are the basis of this book. My hope is that it will show others how to develop the perspective and skills, without undergoing the type of personal crisis that precipitated my changes.

In this book, there are essentially three different priorities:

The first priority is to alter perceptions around being a student and school in general. I will start in Chapter One by describing the illusion of the perfect student. Unfortunately, this illusion is something that is usually unattainable for most people. The first step to becoming a responsible student is destroying the "perfect student" mind trap and focus on the skills and techniques that help you to reach your goals. In Chapter Two, we will discuss how to change your perception of assignments that will make them more enjoyable so you will learn more. How you perceive coursework will greatly affect your willingness to do what it takes and how much you learn. When your perception becomes more positive, you will be more productive and produce higher quality work.

The second priority of this book addresses the skills that students should develop so that they can be successful in their academic and personal goals. One of the biggest challenge students face is not knowing what courses they need to take and how to be successful in them. In Chapter Three, we discuss how to figure out what courses you need to take and how to track your college career to allow the most flexibility for the future. Then, in Chapter Four, we will focus more on how to develop the skills to be successful in each course while exerting the right amount of effort. Having the basic ability of overseeing your own education is not only more beneficial but it also has a positive impact on your advisers and teachers. They are amazed when students understand what they need to do and can carry it out.

Lastly, we will cover navigating inter- and intra-personal conflicts. Frustrations are bound to occur when interacting with others; however, managing these frustrations is essential to be a productive and responsible student. In Chapter Five, we'll cover the major causes of frustrations while focusing on how to identify the specific cause of the issue. We will explore how to solve or manage the frustration so that it does not negatively affect your ability to perform academically. In Chapter Six, we will evaluate interpersonal aspects of school, specifically focused on the why, how, and when to contact your professor to ensure your success in the course.

My goal in this book is to share my own experiences in my many years of being a successful student. My hope is that my experiences will adjust your perspective about being a responsible student and help you to develop skills in navigating college.

THE ILLUSION OF THE PERFECT STUDENT

The illusion of the perfect student is an ideal that students tend to either strive for to their detriment or completely give up the pursuit of it when they realize it is unattainable or unsustainable. While there are many consistent components to this illusion, everyone's idea of the perfect student is different.

For me, the perfect student is one that wakes up around 5 a.m. and studies for a couple of hours. Then, they have a nutritionally balanced breakfast that, of course, they made themselves. Afterward, they head off to their 8 a.m. class because all the perfect students never shy away from 8 a.m. classes! They attend all of their classes and they spend about 3-4 hours in the afternoon studying. They don't take naps through the day because their studies are so important. This person always has a clean desk in their room and regularly spends time in the library. They enjoy some socializing before going to sleep at a reasonable time so they can start their day again tomorrow with energy.

The perfect student always has the most meticulous planner, knowing when all the assignments are due and working diligently on them in smaller sections. Their notes look like the teacher's because they write down everything that is said in class with beautiful legible handwriting. The professors are always amazed by their ability to complete the assignments and how polished their work is. Of course, they always participate in class discussions and are complimented on their keen insight on a topic. They are never stressed about assignments or tests because they started studying and working on them way ahead of the due date. In this way, they complete their schooling with ease and are highly recommended by professors for awards and post-graduate opportunities.

Now, if you want a book about how to become your version of a perfect student, please stop reading and seek out other books that will help you try to become your ideal. After eight years of post-secondary schooling and experiences, I am nothing like my description of the perfect student!

When you begin to think about your description of the perfect student, do you notice that it is the opposite of who you are and your personality?

For me, one of the most significant parts of my description is the ability to wake up early and be productive in the morning. This included taking early morning classes, making and eating a balanced breakfast, and being able to study in the morning. I was not endowed with these attributes; however, my mother, sister, and every other person I surround myself with are almost over-endowed with this ability!

For example, in my first semester of my college sophomore year, my earliest class was at noon, biochemistry. I missed about a third of these classes, often from oversleeping. I would love to be able to justify this by saying that I was up till 4 or 5 a.m. working on assignments from this class, but I generally would go to sleep before midnight on these days. I would easily sleep for ten to twelve hours throughout my college years. I knew deep down that there was never a possibility that I would wake up early to get work done. I didn't eat a balanced breakfast nor would I have not been the one to make it. To the point, I am the antithesis of a morning person!

You may notice that your ideal person in a certain situation is often not in line with who you really are. I see this as a form of self-sabotage that many of us seem to think is good to engage in. You see, once you have accepted that these characteristics are necessary to excel at something, you have prescribed to the belief that to be good at it requires you to completely change who you are.

Unfortunately, you are more likely to decrease your happiness and quality of life in this pursuit. In order to try to fulfill this perfect ideal, you will change your routine or work on these things for a short period of time, become miserable, then give up and say that you are incapable of achieving your goal. If you're like me, you will go through multiple cycles of this where each attempt further confirms the belief that you cannot achieve these ideals.

From your "failed" attempts to become a perfect student, you have cemented the idea that you are simply not a good student. You are now perceiving a skill that takes practice as an innate characteristic that you either have or do not have. If being a good student is an innate characteristic, then no matter how frustrating it is, you believe that you cannot change it. This now becomes your excuse every time you do not do as well as you would like. Unfortunately, all you are doing is limiting yourself and your potential while causing unnecessary disappointment and frustration.

A major component of taking responsibility for your learning is realizing that your ideal of a perfect student is, in fact, an illusion. It is not REAL. Attempting to attain this illusion will generally only result in failure. This does not mean that you should never try to become a better person or stop trying to mature and grow. For example, I shouldn't simply give up on working on becoming a productive morning person. The trick is that I shouldn't tie my ability to be a morning person to my ability to be a good student. I can personally attest that you can be a good student without being a morning person. Instead, you should work with your personality and what attributes you have in order to make yourself a better student.

Through my experiences, I have seen many people who are about to enter college who fully believe that they are going to become their perfect student ideal when they get there. Many people think that this is just going to "happen for" them. They believe they are going to be successful because they are told of all the opportunities just waiting for them if they would just show up.

I remember a friend of mine who was about to start college telling me that he was going to be pre-med, president of the Student Government Association, popular, and be a successful student. I talked with him about how college is never going to match his ideal. Most people are not going to manage and succeed in all these roles simultaneously. He was not this person in high school, but he believed college was going to be different. He believed he was going to fulfill his ideal without any attempts to alter himself. Unfortunately, he did not become this person in college and, unfortunately, did not finish his first year of college.

I think most people have a burning desire to be a different person in some respects. Instead of working step by step to become something like the person we want to be, we attempt to change everything at once and think that we are going to be successful. We tend to put off the things we want to change until another planned big change is going to happen.

For many young adults, this change is going to college or starting a new job. I believe this is often why people become upset, sad, and maybe even depressed a month or two into college or a new job. The idea of forming a habit takes about 21 days of consistent change. Now, if you are trying to change multiple components at the same time, especially when you are combining this with a major transition in your life, it may work until the smallest hurdle challenges your ability to continue. And it usually doesn't take much to stop us! Then all the changes you are working on will fall apart because the stress of maintaining changes is too overwhelming.

Many times, the daily changes you want to make are not actually helpful in garnering the success you want. For me, becoming a morning person was very important to my success in academia. The space in which studying took place was important: a clean desk or the library. The timing of studying was important: twice a day, once in the morning and once in the afternoon. However, none of these things are imperative to becoming a good student. Instead, they were simply the things I did not excel at. They were the deficiencies I saw in my life and I wanted to change them.

I am not a "clean desk" person nor a productive morning person. I am more productive spending long blocks of time intensely working on something rather than working on smaller sections of a project. In fact, the many times I attempted to become this ideal, I was less productive. Attempting to wake up earlier than I needed would result in exhaustion and little desire to work. Breaking up bigger assignments and projects into smaller assignments with regular deadlines usually meant that I would skip multiple weeks of self-defined deadlines and then become more stressed when I had to cram all the work into a smaller time period. I became even more disappointed in myself because I was unable to maintain my new standards that I had set for myself.

By the way, there is no such thing as a perfect student. There is no student that is happy with every part of their academic life in all circumstances. We all experience frustrations and disappointment. Becoming a responsible student is learning how to manage these frustrations that make you a better student instead of allowing them to derail you from your goals. It is important to recognize that even your peers that seem to have it all together will mess up occasionally and become frustrated with their version of themselves.

So how do you work to be a better student in your own way? It is actually simpler than you would think. You start with your strengths, identify your weaknesses, and work step-by-step on improving your weaknesses that stop you from your goals.

Exceptional students are a spectrum of people with different personalities, dreams, and attributes. One of the biggest discussions in becoming a better student is procrastination. Everyone has probably been told not to procrastinate.

Peers and professors say:
    Start working on assignments early.
    Don't wait till the night before a test to cram.

Yet, I have never seen someone who regularly procrastinates suddenly decide to stop procrastinating because someone lectured on the benefits of not procrastinating. On the other hand,

I have seen many procrastinators get stressed out about an assignment or exam and discuss that they have learned their lesson and plan to stop procrastinating! But when the next assignment comes up, they wait till just before it is due to start working on it. Their stressful cycle starts over again.

Does this sound familiar? We are generally told that procrastinating is not a technique employed by good students. However, I know many good students that procrastinate and still produce great work. In fact, many of my peers procrastinate and then impress me with their work. For them, procrastination is not a hindrance to their ability to be a productive student; however, it can just be more stressful than necessary or healthy!

I am not saying that procrastination is a good skill to have. Using procrastination would not be productive for me. In my schoolwork, I have the same habits of a procrastinator where I work intensely on a single project until it is completed and then feel burned out afterward. The difference is that I do this long before the project is due. Most of the time, I have projects finished at least a week (if not weeks) before they are required to be submitted.

This is how I manage my stress level because I am not nearly as productive if I am under a lot of stress and concerned that I may not have the time to finish the project. If a person who is a productive "procrastinator" attempts to adopt my way of completing schoolwork, it is unlikely that they would be very successful. Some people are very good when working under pressure. When the stakes are not as high for them, they do not produce the same quality of work. Therefore, why should they keep attempting to change their strategy just to fail repeatedly?

We've discussed people who are productive procrastinators and people who do not procrastinate; however, there is a third and very important category of students. Those who procrastinate and it hurts their work. These people will generally submit incomplete or low-quality work. Usually, the reason they are submitting this type of work is simply because they did not devote an adequate amount of time to completing it.

If they have a goal to become their ideal student, they will not be able to succeed due to low quality results. It will cause them to believe that they aren't capable of better work. Instead, they should make a goal of better assessing the time required to complete an assignment and working on it ahead of time, which may mean simply starting the assignment a few days earlier than they usually do. Or maybe it is even starting an assignment at the same time as they usually do but ensuring their environment is distraction free when they work on it. The changes that need to be made are usually much simpler and smaller than the extremes people will attempt (and mostly fail) to achieve to meet an ideal.

It is critical to abandon the desire to change drastically in attempts to meet an extreme ideal that most likely would not help you succeed anyway. From changing your perspective, you can focus on making small changes that are going to assist you in becoming a better, more productive student. The rest of this book is going to discuss the major topics that students must grasp to be more productive and produce better work.

TURNING ASSIGNMENTS INTO OPPORTUNITIES

Students see going to college as an opportunity and when they there, they look forward to the opportunities they will have after college. College is often seen as a chore. You must complete a certain number of assignments with a certain GPA for a degree and maybe learn a little something at the same time. Rarely do students feel that what they are learning or the assignments they are performing will assist them in real life. They are simply trying to obtain the credentials proving they took a specific class or have a certain degree. This greatly decreases the enjoyment of school, especially for those that truly want to be competent and knowledgeable in the field they want to contribute in.

Throughout my freshman year of college, coursework was just the annoying assignments I had to complete to pass courses. My work ethic on these courses simply came from my desire to do well; however, the assignments themselves meant very little to me. I thought that I was an excellent student because I had a good GPA, was employed as a tutor, and rarely had any problems with my professors.

Unfortunately, I could not tell you in detail anything from my freshman year classes. However, since my sophomore year, I can tell you in detail about what I learned in most of my classes and even about assignments I completed. This is because I started viewing my assignments differently.

For example, at my college, all sexuality and gender classes were instructed by the same professor. I started taking these classes to fulfill general education requirements. These classes were structured the exact same way. So, once you learned how to do well in one class, you could do well in all her classes with little stress. However, her classes had a substantial amount of high-level work, with papers and tests due every couple of weeks, which were graded according to high standards. She expected you to be capable of creating substantial connections between course concepts and to take responsibility for your own learning. Her assignments were generally vaguely described like "write a film review that connects ideas in the film to concepts from class".

I made the choice of taking two of these classes together in the first semester of my sophomore year: Sexual Minorities and Trans Communities. While the material was fascinating, everyone complained about the amount of work expected of us. At first, it was difficult to understand what she wanted from us due to her descriptions. Again, no matter how many times she explained an assignment, the deliverable of the assignment was always vague. To people who are accustomed to performing chore-like assignments, we had no idea how to perform assignments that were not clearly laid out. The reason why these assignments were so vague was that they allowed you to explore any idea related to the material that you wanted, and you were responsible for the product. However, giving more options to a student usually requires more thought both in quantity and quality of the work.

Taking responsibility for your learning has its advantages and disadvantages. It requires a lot more thought and effort. It eliminates the validity of excuses that would make schooling much easier. However, it also allows you to target your learning where you want it to go. It allows more opportunities and pride of not only your degree or certificate, but also the work that you put into achieving it.

During that semester, there was a substantial amount of time and effort I had to put into those two classes. Despite this, it was an enjoyable and, oddly, a fun time. You see, I was in control of the work I did that semester. I was choosing what I focused on and learned. When I watched films, I thought about the academic nature of those films. This was not only for documentaries, where they are meant to be academic, but also in Hollywood movies. While watching a movie, I could make a connection to the class and then explore that connection. I could justify my stance, beliefs and values while getting credit for an assignment. Through this work, I learned the importance of thinking through a concept instead of trying to figure out the right answer.

The more school I complete, the more I realize the importance of this principle. Exploring a concept and thinking critically about it is a very important skill to possess, especially in academia. It is a skill that requires thought and practice to build up and maintain. Therefore, assignments requiring this are true opportunities to develop the necessary skills. Looking at potentially complex or vague assignments as opportunities can also help you to demonstrate that you can think critically and creatively which then makes the assignments seem more exciting and interesting. They become a manageable challenge instead of a chore. Sometimes, they even become an enjoyable way to spend time and something you might want to talk about with your peers.

When you are taking control of your learning and taking pride in your work, not only does the work seem like an opportunity, but more opportunities usually come your way.

During my sexuality and gender studies classes, there was always a research paper that was assigned in every class. This paper was an 8 to 10-page term-paper with a panel presentation at the end of the semester. For this project, you could choose any topic related to the class topic. While many of my peers saw this as an annoying and hard assignment, I saw it as the ability to study any topic that interested me.

My first semester, I wrote one of these papers in each of my classes. In Trans Communities, I wrote a paper about the challenges and successes in relationships involving trans persons. I was simply interested in what research had previously shown could cause complications in these relationships and what tactics had been shown to increase the success of these relationships.

However, after my professor read my paper, she told me that she wanted to nominate it for the library research paper award. We agreed to further edit and prepare it for submission in a couple months. We worked through a couple of drafts together and prepared the supplemental documents and submitted it.

Later that semester, I was notified that my paper was not selected for this award. I was disappointed, nonetheless. I had placed all that work into my paper for nothing. My first draft of my paper had already received an A in the class. All the additional work I put into the paper was essentially worthless. My professor had spent a significant time working with me on my paper for the reward because she thought that it was worth the effort. In the end though, I could honestly say we were both proud of the work we had done and the final project.

While it sounds good to say I was proud of my work, you might question the legitimacy of my statement that making opportunities and taking pride in your work truly brings you any new opportunities. Fortunately, this story does not end here. For the rest of my college career, I forgot about the paper as it sat in my computer's hard drive.

However, in my second year of graduate school, there was a call for a chapter proposal for an anthology on transgender narratives at my university. I decided to re-examine my old papers that I had written for my college classes. I came across this paper again and considered submitting a chapter proposal based on it. Since my experience with proposing and writing chapters for an anthology was extremely limited, I reached out to my previous sexuality and gender studies professor to ask if she would be willing to assist me in submitting this chapter. She replied that she would help with expanding, rewriting, and submitting a proposal.

At first, I thought this was going to be an easy task to me. Wouldn't it simply be writing a page about what you plan to write in your chapter? As easy as that sounds, for some reason, it is incredibly hard to describe what you plan to talk about in a chapter, while also describing why it is important to talk about each point, in an extremely limited space. After working through the necessary research, writing, and editing on multiple drafts with my collaborator, we finally had a chapter proposal to submit to the editors.

Unfortunately, after submitting a chapter proposal, the real work began writing the chapter. While I had already had a ten-page paper that outlined most of the research that I wanted to present, I decided to work on the manuscript for the chapter from scratch.

Since the chapter proposal deadline was only two months before the manuscript deadline, it was necessary to start working on the chapter prior to the notification of whether the proposal had been accepted or not. Spending time working on something that had already been rejected before in hopes that someone else would want to accept it can be exhausting and frustrating. Given the limited time I had and my other responsibilities as a graduate student, the only way I could have written that chapter was due to the previous research I had done and written four years prior.

About halfway through writing the chapter, I received a notification that the editors had accepted my chapter proposal! After submitting my chapter to the anthology, I was proud and happy about the work I had done four years before. At that time, I never considered that my work on a simple assignment would lead to being an author of a published chapter in an anthology that would be used to teach the same class that I was taking when I wrote the original version! Talk about grasping an opportunity!

Do you now have a good idea of how to change assignments into opportunities especially if they are vague and how you can personalize them?

What about all the assignments that are simply there to solve a list of problems that seem impossible to find the answer that are listed on your professor's answer key? How are these types of assignments really opportunities?

While I spent a large amount of time enjoying writing my papers and giving presentations on interesting topics, I also spent a significant time working on chemistry and physics problem sets. A problem set is only going to help you advance through that class. I'm not going to have any great stories about how I took a problem set and made it into something great outside of that class. Instead, these types of assignments offer opportunities to increase your abilities in the subject.

In my General Physics class, in my sophomore year, each week we had problem sets to complete online. These problem sets included a variety of problems to implement the concepts we were learning in that section of the class. They were generally more analytical and math-based problems than conceptual problems. Therefore, there were about 30-50 problems each week often multiple questions testing the same concept.

Now, if you already think you know these concepts, you might feel like performing these problems is simply wasting your time. On the other hand, if you have no idea how to start working on these problems, completing the problem set feels like an academic brick wall that you could never push through. Through these problem sets, on different types of problems, I endured both experiences. No matter which side of the experience you are on, completing these types of problem sets just seems like a grueling frustration. So how do you change the way you perceive this task?

How does this problem set truly become an opportunity to you?

Answer: You change your goal regarding the task.

Let's start with the second scenario first as I imagine that it is the experience of most students. When you think that a problem set is just more work to show you that you do not understand the material, the first step to overcoming this is to stop, breathe, and start to manage the frustration, something I will cover more later.

Next, look at the problem set as an opportunity to "learn on the job" as it were. With the first problem of a certain concept, search the internet, talk to classmates or your professor, examine your book, or re-examine your notes to slowly work through the problem learning how to complete the problem and learning the concepts themselves.

Then, as you start to proceed through additional problems of the same concept, try to decrease the number of resources you are using to answer the question. The goal is to be able to complete the final question or questions of the problem set for a specific concept with no external resources.

A problem set, that at first might seem like an impossible challenge, can instead become a way to learn and gain confidence though working through the task.

On the other hand, if you feel that you are already understand the concepts and how to implement them, how is completing a problem set on those concepts anything more than just busy work?

Many times, we think we know a concept, but when working through a problem, we might find some points where we get stuck or where we are not as confident.

Even if you are certain that you can complete the problems, why not take the benefit of essentially a pre-test? Use the problem set to work through all the problems with no external resources. It is much better to work through parts that you may get stuck at in a low-risk problem set over a higher-risk test.

The problem sets also gives you the ability to understand the standards of your professor prior to taking a test. For example, in one problem set, I felt somewhat confident in most of the problems on that set. I submitted my assignment expected to get a high score. However, when I received my problem set back graded, I had lost multiple points. I realize that the loss of a few points may not seem like a major penalty, but on a ten-point assignment, it will get your attention!

My first thought was that I clearly did not understand one of the concepts. After review of my problem set, there were no fundamental errors in the concepts or in the math. Unfortunately, I did not know that my professor required all answers to be reported in units adhering to the International System of Units or SI units. SI units are units like meters or centimeters instead of feet or inches. In this case, I reported my units similar to the units presented in the questions of the various problems, which were not always SI units. Therefore, the problem set gave me the opportunity to understand what my professor wanted so that I did not lose additional points on important tests.

Ultimately, a major change that students must undergo to truly be able to take responsibility for their learning is to change their perception of classwork. We have all viewed coursework and assignments as chores that are just there to take up our time.

However, when we alter our thinking to view our coursework as our job and each assignment is a new opportunity to explore a new topic, we to learn how to implement a concept and gain confidence by working through problems. When you alter your perspective, you may suddenly realize that the work isn't such a chore. Instead, you might start to become excited about your coursework which will cause you to produce higher quality work in less time.

KNOWING WHAT YOU NEED TO DO

Once you start viewing your coursework as an opportunity, you may get excited about your potential and the discoveries you'll make. However, the first step to completing the work is knowing what you need to do and in what order. In college, knowing what you need to do is not as simple as following a list of courses or assignments. So, we'll go through the different levels where it is important to know what you need to do starting with which courses to take.

Many of my friends have told tell me stories about how they took useless classes just because they didn't know what they needed in order to graduate! We have all thought some classes were useless at one point or another, but usually the course is meeting specific requirements that is required to obtain our degree. Unfortunately, there are many students who are taking classes that are not even counting for any requirements to graduate.

You might question how this can happen, "Is it not simple to figure out which courses one needs or doesn't need?". The answer is both yes and no. While the information about what classes are required for general education, majors, and minors is public information, it is the students' responsibility for finding and registering in the right classes.

I can remember discussions with my peers in college detailing the process of how they chose classes. They would talk with their academic advisor who would tell them what classes they should sign up for based on the <u>advisor's</u> experience. Then, they would register for those courses. Pretty simple and on the path to success, right?

In my case, my freshman academic advisor did not which courses were required for my major and did not even think about seeking courses that could possibly count for multiple requirements.

When I began college, I knew I wanted to be a chemistry major. For my first college semester, I was scheduled to take a general chemistry course. I had scored a 4 on the Advanced Placement (AP) Chemistry exam in high school. I made a 5 on the AP Psychology exam and was interested in pursuing the subject as a possible minor.

Even though, my high school did not let me know if my AP credits could count toward any required courses, I examined the academic catalog and found that my college accepted AP exam scores of 4 or higher in lieu of general requirements. So, I contacted the college's registrar's office and submitted the paperwork showing I scored a 4 or higher on the Chemistry AP and Psychology AP exams. In my submission, I asked what credit I would be offered for my exam scores and what courses I would be allowed to place out of.

A few days later, I received a response from the school. I would be allowed to place out of general chemistry 1 and 2! And, I would be allowed to place out of the lecture for psychology as a natural science where I would only have to take the lab portion of the class.

I went from taking General Chemistry my first semester in college to starting in Organic Chemistry that semester! As a freshman, I was in the chemistry sequence with the sophomore class, which is the only reason I was able to finish my degree in four years. If I had not been willing to read the academic catalog and determine where I could get credits in advance of starting college, I would not have been given the chance to place out of certain courses which accelerated my college career.

Lesson one in college: You need to look for ways to advance your career because **no one is going to do it for you**.

What if you do not have any options to place out of courses, how do you figure out which courses to take?

It is important from the beginning to be honest with yourself about what you want out of college and what work you want to do after college. The biggest decision will be what major you want to pursue. What contribution do you want to make to the world and what field provides opportunities to contribute?

In the beginning of college, it is fine if you are unsure of what major you are interested in. If I was unsure of what I wanted to do after college, I would:

- Choose one to two majors that have piqued my interest
- Examine the introductory courses for each of the majors and choose to take between one to three courses (to assist in deciding which major to pursue)
- Discover how many of the general education requirements would be fulfilled taking the introductory courses.

If you can explore your interests while earning general education requirements, you will confidently choose a major earlier in college and possibly take classes that are allowing you to fulfill multiple requirements.

Students who do not finish school with the major they started with often take longer to graduate, especially when they make a change in major much later. The students I have known that have changed their major usually start college with a focus on a specific major. However, many of these students were not truly confident in the major they had chosen but decide to stick with their major until at least their sophomore year. After a quarter of their time in college, they change their major which is completely understandable but they are now starting over. Usually, three to five classes that they have taken will not fulfill any requirements for the new major! That's about a whole semester of courses. You need to be honest with yourself as early and as often as possible. Allow yourself to explore additional opportunities and be open to what find and make new decisions.

When you have decided on a major, it is important to research and constantly be aware of your progress towards your desired degree in terms of what courses to take and the level of success you are experiencing. One of my friends found out in her senior year that she did not have enough credits to graduate on time. She had been told by an advisor that one course would count for a general education requirement, but it had been taken off that requirement a year before she had started there. So, she had to figure out a new method for meeting all her requirements with only one semester left before she planned on graduating. Talk about **STRESS**!

Unfortunately, this is a very common story. I have heard from many students that they took or did not take classes on an advisor's or professor's word and it later became an issue before graduation. However, with a little extra effort on your part, you can create a more efficient path to your degree and increase your confidence in your plan ensuring that you are meeting all requirements of the school, degree, major, and minors you are pursuing. It is your life and career anyway and remember that no one is going to do it for you!

BASIC LOGISTICS TO EFFICIENT COURSEWORK PLAN

Being willing to perform the extra work of planning your courses will not get you far if you have no idea how to determine what your coursework should be. While learning the requirements and planning your classes is relatively simple, colleges tend to spend little to no time educating students on these logistical topics.

Basic logistics of how to develop an efficient coursework plan:

1. The first thing to do no matter what college you are going to or what major you are pursuing is to find and familiarize yourself with an updated/current academic catalog or bulletin. Usually, you can find this document by searching for it on your college or universities website. If you are not able to find it, contact your registrar's office or examine their web page and they will be

able to give you either an electronic or physical copy.

2. In the academic catalog, all the requirements for general education, majors, minors, and certificate courses are outlined. The first step is to outline or write out the general education requirements and your major requirements. If you are set on having a minor as well, I would also write out those requirements; however, it is possible that you may decide on a minor after looking at the courses you are planning on taking.

3. List which general education requirements are met by courses required by your major. There tends to be elective courses that you give you some choices in which classes you take in every major. For electives, it is a good idea to first examine the possible courses for those that meet your interest. Then, to meet the other elective requirements, look for courses that will fulfill additional general education requirements that you do not currently have.

4. Next, examine the prerequisites for each of the courses you have planned for your major. Typically, there are courses that build on the introductory level courses and require the previous classes to be taken beforehand. In making a coursework plan, note which courses need to be taken as prerequisites.

5. Now, fill in a four-year plan with your major courses making sure that your prerequisites are in place prior to the classes that need them.

6. Next, add placeholders to your four-year plan for general education requirements. Evaluate classes that fulfill general education requirements to find ones that you are interested in and for those that can meet more than one requirement, if your school allows it.

7. During your first year, you will most likely be fulfilling many of your general education requirements with a few of your major requirements. This means that you will be taking a variety of courses from many different disciplines. In this case, you might find a discipline that you want to continue studying, but don't desire to change your major or pursue a second major. In this case, it is a good idea to plan to meet the minor requirements for this

discipline. In your four-year plan, you should intersperse these requirements. The same tips from your major apply to your minor:

(1) make sure you are planning the necessary prerequisites and

(2) make sure you know which courses will count for general education requirements.

Using these tips, you should be able to meet all requirements and at the same, not take unnecessary courses that meet your purpose.

8. Periodic evaluation of your plan at the beginning and end of every semester is just as important as making an initial plan. In addition to a four-year plan, you should keep a list of all classes you need to take for your degree(s). Some of these courses can be ambiguous, such as General Education Requirement #1. Then each semester, you should update this list to include completed, in-progress, and future coursework. Updating this list will allow you to have flexibility in your plan depending on when courses are offered.

Doing this work yourself does not mean you no longer use the resource of your academic advisor. Instead, the best practice is to come to your advisor with this work completed. Then, the advisor can review your plan and give you some suggestions on the timeline or what courses to take. This will not only increase your confidence, but it will also display your organizational and self-motivational skills to your advisor. In the future, your advisor may be a good reference with the ability to highlight these skills and set you apart from the typical student.

My undergraduate career was possible due to my initiative to perform this work independently. I was a double major, triple minor, and received an advanced leadership certificate. In addition, I was in a school that required at least 66 credits for general education requirements. I finished all the requirements within four years. I was able to accomplish this simply because I always had a plan, worked the plan and analyzed it for possible issues. The plan changed drastically over time. However, because I was always reviewing and updating it, I had the flexibility to add a second major halfway through my college career.

Prior to my first college class, I was familiarized with the academic catalog and was aware of the requirements both for my planned major and for the general education requirements. I ensured that I was taking all the courses in my first year that would allow me the greatest flexibility in the future by taking the prerequisite courses for my major with taking general education requirements.

Each semester, I would spend an hour or two analyzing my four-year plan to ensure that I was still on track to graduate. Every time the course offerings for the next semester came out, I would look at the courses that were time sensitive first (i.e. prerequisites or major courses rarely offered) and planned to register for them first. Then, with the credits that I had left to fulfill, I examined which courses being offered that would meet the general education requirements that I still needed.

My academic advisors required meetings every semester to discuss the progress toward the degree and plan the classes for the next semester. I always went into these meetings with a planned list of courses and my updated four-year plan. My advisors were always pleasantly surprised that I had already performed the work that the meeting was for! Later, when my advisors wrote reference letters for graduate schools that I applied to, they were able to discuss my excellent organizational and planning skills and how I took accountability for my future.

While taking responsibility for my learning was beneficial for proving that I could be organized, there was a larger benefit. Since I put in the initial work and planning, I never had to question or feel uncertain that there was something missing from my plan. Or worse, that my advisor and I had misunderstood each other as many students have experienced.

I was always confident and stress-free about how quickly I could graduate and what all I could accomplish in my time in college. Taking responsibility for knowing and taking the required courses reduced my stress and ensured that there were no surprises later in my college career. I saw my fellow classmates go through those stresses and I saw how it negatively affected them, both mentally and in their careers.

My greatest tip to all college students is to take responsibility with your coursework plan, review it often, and make adjustments as needed. You will be grateful for the reduced stress and the increased confidence in your future!

NAVIGATING EACH COURSE TO SUCCESS

Now that you have taken the time to become confident in your coursework plan, you must take the classes and understand what you need to do in each class. The importance of this understanding is that it is personalized to you. So, this will include planning the assignments that are required for the course but, even more important, is to understand everything that will be required of you during the class. Once you have a good idea of what is expected, you can plan how to meet those requirements and complete your coursework with less stress.

The first step is to analyze the syllabus for each course. The syllabus is going to tell you the concrete items you will have to produce and submit. Each semester, either prior to the start of the semester or during the first week, I examined the assignments, papers and exams and their timeline for completion.

Early in my college career, I would write down all the assignments in a planner so that I could make sure that I would not forget any of them. However, as time went on, I stopped using a planner all together. Even though I would take time to writing assignment details into my planner, I never used my planner to keep track of them as they were due.

I would write regular "To Do" lists which something I still do today. Whatever method that works for you to organize your thoughts and assignments, it is important to familiarize yourself with what will be required of you for multiple reasons:

- First, it is important to make sure you are not forgetting

to complete assignments on time.
- Second, knowing the assignments early in the semester ensures that you can plan the amount of time you need for assignments and when you should start them.
- Third is possibly the most overlooked reason: knowing the type of assignments you need to do should change the way you learn the material. For example, if you know that your main assignments are tests, you may plan to spend your class and study time focused on studying for a test. However, if your main assignments are papers or take-home exams, then you may spend your study time and class time differently, possibly taking on more interactive roles or focused on implementing the information you learn in class.

FINDING THE CLASS RHYTHM

After you know what assignments are required, you can start understanding what you need to do in each course. The first thing is to figure out the class "rhythm". Most professors will have a strategic timeline in the class where assignments are due on a specific day or there will be a regular time distance between assignments and tests. Once you figure out the rhythm of the class, you can plan how and when you need to put in effort to complete assignments and be successful.

I have taken highly well-structured classes and classes that were completely unstructured; however, from my experience, I found that is a general rhythm in all my classes. My sexuality and gender studies classes are an example of a very structured class. They were structured into five modules and each module contained a quiz that would be due on a Sunday night toward the end of the module. In each module, we had to complete a film review where we would watch a film and discuss how the film related to topics covered in the class. There was always a major project due for the semester which was an 8 to 10 page research paper on a topic related to the course. Occasionally, there would be an additional presentation or other assignment throughout the semester that was not part of the typical module structure.

For these classes, I knew that besides attending lectures, there was no "regular" work that I needed to complete on a weekly basis. I would read some of the assigned readings during the week here and there. But to be truthful, I usually don't complete the assigned readings unless I know that I need to do so to be successful in the class. So, I used my time and focused my attention toward the assignments that were due.

For these classes, the quizzes were online and even though they were timed, I generally had enough time to refresh my memory of the required information, if needed. As a result, I rarely studied for the quizzes and would instead study while I was taking the quiz.

Then, I would work on my film review shortly after watching the film. I usually spent less than two hours to write and submit a film review and I usually received an A grade for my reviews. For me, success in this was because I started and finished the requirement right after I watched the film. It was a timing thing as much as it was singular focus on one task.

The final project could be a bit trickier on deciding how to complete it. The final project would usually have minor assignments in each module. This was helpful to ensure that we did not lose track of the major assignment. In this case, from the beginning of the semester, I would consider what topic I would write my paper on and generally finalizing it a week before it was due.

Then, I would gather research and outline the final project over time. Finally, I would complete the project a couple weeks prior to the due date.

For these classes, after the first week, it was straightforward in what I needed to do each week to be successful. However, for some of my classes, there was not an outline for the class. In one of my classes, the assignments were predominately papers or proposals. The syllabus had four proposals assigned with two of those being edits and re-writes of the previous proposals. However, by the end of the course, we had written over six proposals with only one being rewritten. The topics for each proposal were usually given to us less than a week before the proposal was due!

A proposal is a document where you present a new area of research that has not been done before. You have a rather short space to present your research idea and the methodology behind it. Proposals are required in scientific fields in order to receive funding to conduct research. Normally, you are an expert in the field writing a proposal to fund real research you plan to complete. In this case, we were barely given the basic knowledge in the field and on our own, we had to:

- Learn and understand a topic
- Discover what research had been already conducted on the topic
- Arrive at a completely original research idea
- Write a proposal explaining our research idea, how we would conduct the research, and what the hypothetical research would achieve.

It was required to complete the proposals in less than a week and they would be critiqued in class by both our peers and our professor!

Even under ideal conditions, writing a quality proposal is a stressful experience, but with the rapid pace and extreme expectation placed on the students, these assignments seemed impossible to complete. As a result, for the first couple of weeks, I felt overwhelmed and it seemed that passing the class was impossible. Initially, my way of dealing with the it was to complain, and I'd seriously considered withdrawing from it. Unfortunately, it was a class that was required.

So, I decided I had to figure out how to be successful in the course despite how frustrating or annoying it was. By reviewing the class "rhythm", I learned that during most of the semester, not much work was required. However, about every two to three weeks, I would have to spend about three solid days understanding the topic and determining what research had already been conducted. While I worked to understand the topic, I would always be looking at how this topic could relate to my interests and any new research I thought could be pursued. After about a day of doing research and understanding the topic, I would have a grasp on the new idea I wanted to write my proposal on.

The next two days were focused on writing the proposal while still researching the idea. The proposal consisted of background, hypothesis, specific aims, and conclusion/significance. Before I wrote the proposal, I outlined my hypothesis and specific aims. Then, I could write my proposal and submit it before the deadline.

Once I learned how to write proposals, passing the class did not seem impossible anymore. Instead of complaining and wanting to give up every time we were assigned a proposal, I learned how to use the "rhythm" and understand what I needed to do. This greatly decreased my stress level which is very important to me.

While this class had no real structure (and it did not follow the structure it had in the syllabus), I was successful. The difference was my mindset, my acceptance of the course requirements, and my commitment to my goals. What other people did to be successful in that class could be completely different than what I did. You need find the "rhythm" and use it to your advantage.

BEST WAY TO COMPLETE EACH ASSIGNMENT ... ON TIME, WITH REDUCED STRESS

After you figure out the rhythm of the class, it is important to understand the best way for you to complete each assignment. For some people, it makes more sense to study or work on assignments each week. Other people will prefer to wait and work in large amounts every few weeks instead. Neither of these ways are the correct way to complete a class for every student. Instead, the way that makes you a successful student is the correct way. The way work is completed may differ between people or even between classes.

Think about class work like paying for car insurance. With car insurance, you can choose to pay every month, quarter, or six months. Depending on a person likes to manage their finances, he or she may prefer a large bill only twice a year. On the other hand, another may need to budget a smaller expense every month. The same idea works with deciding how to perform the necessary work in the classroom.

Based on your personality, you may want to have a regular weekly schedule and work on each class every week. For example, I had one friend who spent 3 hours each day in the library working on her coursework. She regularly maintained this despite the amount of work she had in each class that week. In a week where her schoolwork was lighter, she would get ahead, especially on semester-long projects. Then, when the schoolwork was heavier, she was usually ahead on some of the work so she could still complete the requirements for the week within her planned work time. Therefore, choosing to work consistently every week was successful for her and can be successful for others; however, it is not the only work schema that is successful for all students.

On the other extreme, I had a different friend in graduate school that was also a successful student. She completed every assignment within 24 hours of the due date. She tells others and suggest to herself that she should start her assignments much earlier than the due date. Shortly after meeting her, I realized all these comments were all hypothetical and she would not begin her work until right before she needed to have it done.

While we did not have the same work styles, but we both produced about the same quality of work in all aspects of graduate school except in research. This was because there were either no or irregular deadlines for research in our lab. She would prepare research when her advisor would suggest dates or meetings where he expected it to be completed and she would meet these deadlines. Since she was not excited about her research and there weren't real deadlines, she did not move through it as quickly.

Therefore, successful students can be a spectrum of a variety of intellects and work routines. Find out what works best with your time and goals for each course.

KNOWING WHAT TO DO, AND WHAT NOT TO WASTE TIME ON

It is important to know what you need to do in each class despite what your personality would lead you to do. For example, in my abnormal psychology class, we had pop quizzes every week. Even though I was accustomed to only studying for classes right before tests, I had to alter my normal pattern and re-examine my study habits for this class. To meet the new challenge of pop quizzes, I would review the notes from the previous class the night before the next class period. The quick review would give me the ability to get high grades on the multiple-choice pop quiz, if they occurred the next day. Because of review was quick instead of a lengthy cram-session, I did not waste much time if we did not have a quiz the next day.

This brings me to another important point about knowing what you need to do: don't waste time and effort on things you do not need to do.

My suggestion here will most likely be disagreed with by many teachers, but this is based on my own experiences and the experiences of the wide variety of students I have been able to observe throughout my career. It is important to know what work you do **not** need to do to succeed in a class.

I think this is particularly important when it comes to the topic of reading the textbook for a class. To illustrate my point, I took two classes in a recent semester. One course was in endocrinology and another course in women and gender studies. Both courses required a substantial amount of reading each week. However, the way I completed each of these classes was very different despite the similar requirements.

For my endocrinology class, we were told that we were responsible for all the information in the textbook on quizzes and tests. We had an online quiz for every section, but we were given unlimited attempts to complete the quiz. After reading half of the first chapter and attempting to complete the quiz, I found that reading the book was not getting me any closer to getting a perfect score on the quizzes. So, I switched to reviewing the slides the professor had prepared for her lectures and then taking the quiz. I started achieving higher scores on the quizzes. I discovered that generally all the graded assignments, including quizzes and tests, only tested material from her lectures or specific readings she posted online. This meant that I could not only survive but succeed in the class, even though I did not read the textbook that was supposed to be essential to our success. The trade-off was that the quizzes may require a few more attempts to be able to complete with perfect scores. However, the time it would take to attempt the quiz multiple times would not compare to the amount of time it would take to read the book.

At the end of the course, I ended up with an A+ despite not reading the textbook. I knew that to be successful on the quizzes and the tests, I needed to learn the information that my professor had focused on in her lectures and in peer-reviewed articles that were posted. For the peer-reviewed articles, I could typically read the abstracts and skim the figures to gain the information needed to participate in lectures and pass the tests. In fact, the majority of the information on the tests was covered several times in the lectures in class. The most productive time I spent "studying" for the class was when I simply paid attention during the lectures that were required for me to attend. Understanding what I needed to do and know what tasks were not necessary saved me a lot of time and allowed me to succeed.

The women's and gender studies course was quite a different story. In this class, there were no lectures; instead, we had discussions on the readings every week. Once a month, we had to choose a reading and write a response paper about it prior to the day we discussed it. Clearly, I would not become very successful in this class if I avoided readings each week!

In the beginning of the class, I became overwhelmed with the amount of reading each week; however, after about two weeks, I decided what my goals were for each week and learned how to make each reading successful. Since my professor posted all the readings online for the entire semester, each month I would look over the titles of the different readings for that month and then decide which was interesting to me. I knew I had to read this reading early in the weekend before we would be discussing it in class. Then, over the weekend, I would write and submit the response paper. This ensured that I was able to successfully meet this requirement.

Over the rest of the class, I knew I needed to have a good idea of the content in most of the readings (not all of the readings) to manage the discussions in the classroom. During the first couple weeks, I read all the readings assigned spending approximately six to eight hours to complete. During the discussions, I noticed that we could not discuss several readings that were assigned each week. Occasionally, we would split into small groups and summarize a random reading assigned to us. But the amount of time I spent on readings did not correlate to the amount of time and quality of discussions in the classroom.

I had to balance reading enough to be able to have an informed discussion, but not spend an unreasonable amount of time on reading where it made no sense. As a result, I would skim over all the readings picking out a certain quote or theme that I could expand upon in a discussion. But the readings that seemed particularly interesting, I would read a bit more in-depth.

So, in general discussion time, I could maintain a conversation or quickly summarize any given reading. Then, I had the ability to go in-depth on one or two readings of my interest. Because of this method, I appeared as being prepared and engaged while meeting the necessary requirements. But more importantly, I reduced the amount of time reading in half - from six to eight hours a week to two to four hours! At the end of this class, I received an A and never received lower than an A on any grade including participation.

It is very important to learn what you need and **not** need to do to be successful in each class. This includes understanding what assignments and type of work is expected. It is also important to learn what you need to do to successfully complete these assignments. It is crucial to know what <u>suggested</u> work you need to do and how to complete it. For this reason, the advice I gave is not that you should never read the textbook. Instead, it is important to know what you personally need to complete to be able to be an engaged student and be successful in the class.

MANAGING THE FRUSTRATION

Every student has gone through the frustrations of being a student. These frustrations are experienced when students feel that it is impossible to understand a concept, when it seems that professors are not following what the student expects, or when the student believes the work they put forth is their best, but their grade does not reflect it.

These frustrations can be real and valid. When frustrations are not well managed, it can lead to negative feelings of being overwhelmed thinking that the only option left is to give up on succeeding in a course and, possibly, in college. Learning to manage the frustration can not only reduce the feeling of being overwhelmed but can also help you to succeed in a class that seems impossible to pass.

Each type of frustration needs to be managed in its own way but there is a common theme to managing all student-centered frustrations. One major cause of frustration is the feeling that everything is out of your control, that everything is happening to you and you cannot do anything to change the results of what is happening. The trick to realize and accept what things you can and cannot control. Then, focus on what you can control in a class and do the things you can do. Let go of what you cannot control.

To do this, you must realize that any one grade, assignment, or class does not decide anything regarding who you are or what your future potential is.

Many students believe that if they do not receive perfect

grades then people will think less of them or they will not be able to achieve their goals. I tutored several students in organic chemistry that struggled with the class and would exclaim their frustration that if they did not do well in this class then they would never be able to get into medical school. The ability to succeed in a class will decline when a student becomes frustrated and fully believes that their future is reliant upon their success in that one class.

Therefore, it is important to realize that no matter what your future plans are, if you get a B or C or lower in a single class or on a single assignment, it does not make a difference in your overall success. Being a graduate student in chemistry, some of my peers received C's or even failed courses. They retook the chemistry class in their undergraduate career and are still able to pursue a Ph.D. in chemistry. It is important to remember, especially at the bachelors' level, that your desires for your future can change and most future career options do not require bachelor's in a particular field, including graduate school. Instead of becoming overwhelmed, realize that the point of each class is to learn.

For each of the different types of frustrations, there are different things within and out of your control. One of the most common student frustrations is when a student is trying to learn a concept and cannot understand it. With this type of frustration, you cannot control the way a professor chooses to teach a certain topic. However, you can control your reactions to the professor's teaching.

What many people do not realize is that learning the material and concepts is in your control despite how the teacher decides to instruct. Therefore, while complaining about the professor's decisions mar feel beneficial to your mood, it is not an excuse for you to not understand the material. This fact is very hard to hear especially when you are dealing with negativity and exasperation. But the fact is you are responsible for what you learn even more than the teacher is responsible for what and how they teach.

There are plenty of inadequate teachers but students that stand out will succeed despite the prevalence of bad teachers.

Sometimes the problem is not the quality of the teacher but that the structure of the class is not best suited for your learning style. Either way, you must understand the underlying annoyance and learn how to be successful in each class despite the issue.

I was in this scenario in my last class of college. At my college, we had a semester called May Term, where you took up to four credits in about three weeks at the end of the spring semester before graduation. In my last May Term, I had to take an electronics course to finish my physics minor. In this class, there were no lectures. Instead, the class ran from 9 a.m. to 5 p.m., where every day we worked on either a homework or a lab assignment, which had to be submitted the next day. For our labs, we had an oral exam where we were asked specific questions. If something did not work correctly, we would be questioned about it. We could work in groups of 5-6 people. However, especially in stressful situations, working with groups can become extremely difficult.

The first night of this course was one of my lowest moments in college. I questioned my capability to be a successful student and my intellect as a person. I remember sitting in a group work room in the library with my group members staring at a homework assignment amazed by my lack of preparedness. I had no clue how to even begin approaching these homework problems and felt like the I had made some wrong turn in my academic journey.

My frustration on this night was two sided. I was frustrated that I was being expected to perform work with no guidance and background. My frustration extended to the feeling that my own intellect was not substantial enough to handle the workload. About halfway through the night, I realized that I could either let my frustration overcome me and make me useless for attempting to work on the assignment or I could recognize the situation I was in, accept it, and attempt my best at completing the assignment. I chose the second option and by the end of the night, we had completed the assignment to the best of our ability.

I learned in this class that if I started these assignments expecting to know nothing about the topic, I could then use the problems to target my research to find out how to solve the problems. By the end of the course, I earned a perfect score on the final exam and an A in the course.

This course could have been a disaster for me at the end of my college career. I could have easily let the frustration and feelings of hopeless limit my ability to be productive which would have had serious consequences for my career. From the first night, I remember feeling choked with my thoughts of unfairness that this course represented; I was on my own to accomplish a great deal of work in an area I was not comfortable in. Yet, it was the opportunity I needed because it challenged me in a new way. I gained the experience that I can complete work independently and turn what feels like a hopeless situation into a great success. This would have never happened if I could not manage my frustration and find a way to focus on doing what I can do be successful.

While describing why managing your frustration is important, understanding how to manage frustration is very difficult and is, often, very personal. From my experiences, most frustration arises from feelings of unfairness and loss of control or hopelessness. When these frustrations arise, it is important to realize what is within and outside of your control. What is outside of your control must be accepted and not dwelt upon. What is outside your control cannot be used as an excuse to why you didn't do well.

Common elements out of student's control are structure of the class, the teaching style of the professor, or if the teacher likes you or plays favorites. Too often, I hear from my classmates that the only reason they are not successful in a class is because the teacher does not like them or that they are not a good teacher. No matter what a teacher thinks about you, if you perform well in a class, the teacher cannot demolish your grade.

Performing well in these situations is often a factor of taking more work on yourself and being more independent in your learning. While these situations are difficult, they also allow you to grow as a person if you accept the challenge, which will allow you to have continued successes inside and outside the classroom.

REACHING OUT, BUT NOT TOO MUCH

While taking classes, everyone experiences difficulties, but an important part of breaking through these difficulties is being able to reach out to those who listen and can help. Reaching out takes a variety of forms in why, how, and when you are reaching out.

Often, I have seen my classmates intimidated and scared to reach out to anyone when experiencing difficulties in their classes. These often come from an idea that reaching out gives the perception of being unintelligent coupled with a concern for bothering people. There were countless times that my friends would encounter difficulties and I would suggest reaching out to the professor, classmates, or previous students that have taken the class. About 95% of the time, they would have an excuse for not contacting those who could help and attempting everything alone. This affected their grades, stress level, effectiveness as a student, and their capability to learn.

On the other hand, I have experience as a teaching assistant both in my undergraduate and graduate programs, which gives me an understanding for the other side of students reaching out for help. There is such a thing as reaching out too much and it often causes frustration for the teacher producing a tense student-teacher relationship.

In fact, the more that students reach out about information that has already been given to them or extraneous information tangentially related to the class, generally the less likely that they will receive a response. If my email inbox is constantly filling up with students' emails coupled with all of the other emails I receive, I am much more likely to respond to a well-composed email from a student that reaches out with important questions, than I would a confusing email from a student who is constantly contacting me regarding subjects they should already have the answers to.

It is essential to understand what are good reasons, when, and how should you reach out to your teachers.

WHY CONTACT YOUR PROFESSOR

So, let's start with reasons for contacting a teacher. The best way to explain this category is by detailing the DOs and DON'Ts:

Do not email your teacher introducing yourself before the first class. If you will be there on the first day, you can introduce yourself to them then.

Do email your teacher if you are going to be absent for the first class of the semester.

Do read the syllabus first before sending an email to ask a question. This is one of the very frustrating emails to get and I usually do not respond, or I reply by attaching a syllabus with the text of "See attached".

Do include the part of the syllabus that you need clarification on in your email. This helps to show that you have read the syllabus. When syllabus questions come up, the teacher assumes that the student has not read it and dismisses the question showing their frustration with the student. So, it is important to demonstrate to teachers that you do know what the syllabus says when asking questions.

Do contact other students in the class prior to emailing the professor, if possible or applicable. Potentially, other members of your class may have the answer to your question or maybe they have the same questions as you. Either way, contacting classmates first could solve your problem or give you solidarity in your question.

The most valid reasons to reach out in a course is generally a logistical clarification or a content question or misunderstanding. While logistical questions are generally easy to answer, it is important that you do your research prior to contact.

However, for content questions, there are several important considerations prior to contacting a professor. First consider whether you have a defined question or if you are simply confused about a topic. Both situations are valid and worth contacting your professor, but they require different tactics.

If you have a defined question, it would be appropriate to email this question to your professor; however, be prepared that you may not get a direct answer. Sometimes, teachers want to check your understanding and would rather have a conversation about it rather than only responding in an email. However, if there are multiple emails being received on the same topic, a teacher may decide it is best to address the entire class and re-teach a particular topic. So, do not be quickly discouraged if you do not receive the response you were expecting.

If you are confused about a topic without a very specific question, it is best to email a professor requesting meeting rather than asking them to explain the concept to you. Recognize that the professor's time is valuable and that teaching classes accounts for about 30% of their responsibilities. Even though a teacher is not responsible for your learning and they should be helpful, they are not your only resource for understanding the material.

WHEN TO CONTACT PROFESSORS

Now that you have a reason to contact your professor, it is important to consider when and how to contact them. When you contact a professor can have a high impact on whether you receive a response and on the quality of the response. To determine when to contact them, you should consider when you need the information. If you need the information within the next 24 hours, then that moment should become a teaching moment, because you are not likely to get that information that quickly.

The timing of asking questions is one reason why you want to make sure you read the syllabus and be focusing about 1-2 weeks out during the course. If you are ahead, then you will have plenty of time to ask your questions in multiple ways, not rushing your professor. This helps to develop the perception that you are an organized planner. Even when you have plenty of time to ask a question, the timing of your contact can still be very significant.

Most professors work during the normal business day. When they do work outside business hours, there is very low likelihood that they are working to answer students' emails. Professors are constantly being bombarded by emails; therefore, checking emails every time they come into their inbox would be very counterproductive for completing their other responsibilities.

With these two factors, there are two likely fates for an email that is sent outside business hours:

(1) the email is checked by a professor, not responded to, and then is lost because it has already been read or

(2) the email is not checked by the professor and is lost by the next time they check their email in all the additional emails they have gotten since then.

Either way, the likeliness that you get the information you need after emailing a professor late at night or outside business hours is generally low.

Also, the frequency of your contact with professors can be very off-putting. Constantly receiving emails from a student can be frustrating to a professor and lead them to ignore all emails from that student. It is important to limit emails to what is important and relevant.

If you have several questions at a given time, it is best to compile them all into a single email. Questions that can wait to be asked in the next class should be. It is critical to your success to acquire information early and through independent routes first; then reach out to your professor.

HOW TO CONTACT PROFESSORS

Knowing why and when to contact your professor is great, but to have productive contact, how you contact your professor can be just as important. How you contact includes multiple aspects including the medium, the attitude, and the structure of the contact. The two most common mediums for contact are email or in-person conversation.

In this section we are going to focus on email communication, since my experience has shown that it is one of the most difficult options for students to navigate. Emails have a very specific format and, yet, I am always amazed by the types of emails I receive from students.

Often, these emails include ambiguous or, worse, no subject line. There are rarely greetings at the beginning of the email and often there is not enough information for me to understand what the student is asking. It is astounding to me how truly rude people can be in emails. For these reasons, we'll discuss the different facets of writing an email that will create both a good perception of you and give you the information you need.

Let's start with the subject line of an email. The subject line will determine if a professor will even open the email or not because this is what they read first. In the subject line, you should mention the class that the question relates to so that the professor understands the context of the question before opening the email. I generally start my subject with the class number followed by a colon and then the subject of my email. The subject of your email should be concise and express the intent of your email.

Avoid subjects like: Question for class, Confusion on Assignment, or sentences conveying your question. If your questions are about the logistics of an assignment or class, the subject should discuss the assignment or part of the class it is related to and briefly what the question is about.

For example, if there is a question on the deadline for Paper II in a class numbered PSYC 210, I would write a subject as PSYC 210: Paper II Deadline. Having a concise, accurate subject line informs your professor of what the content is and the importance of the email. This also helps him to know how long the response will take.

After creating a good subject line, next comes the body of

the email. It is always respectful to start a message with a greeting. The greeting can vary but should be respectful. In the Virginia Women's Institute for Leadership, we are taught to greet with the appropriate time of the day, i.e. Good Morning or Good Afternoon. There are other greetings such as Dear Professor Name or Dear Dr. Name that are fine as well. However, not including a greeting suggests a level of informality that is not consistent with the majority of student/professor relationships. Therefore, this can often be perceived as a sign of disrespect by some professors causing them to be terse in their response or not respond at all.

After typing a greeting, the rest of the body of your email should also be well organized and detailed. It is important to include all the necessary information in the email for the professor to understand but do not include irrelevant information.

I remember getting emails that were vague to the point that I had no idea what assignment or topic the student was talking about. Remember that teaching a class is only a portion a professor's responsibilities. While the subject matter is clear and fresh in your mind, the professor may need to be reminded of the specifics to understand your question.

Conversely, I have received many emails that gave too many details and took too long to get to the point. One time, I got an email from a student that was struggling in the class asking me what they needed to do. There were no specific questions, just a page's worth of text telling me that they did not understand what they were doing wrong in the class and that I should inform them specifically of what they needed to do. Then, the student continued about how they were a great student and they shouldn't be having problems in the course. While I completely understand the frustrations of not succeeding in a course, there is never a situation where you need to email your professor telling them your story to prove you are a good student and then request an individualized notification and syllabus for every assignment.

If you are struggling in a class, the best way for discussing this with your professor is in person. Using email is a good way to set up a meeting, but the actual conversation should occur in person.

Lastly, this example brings up my last important point regarding contacting professors. Despite the frustration you might feel, contacting your professor in a disrespectful way is never productive. Even if you feel like the reason you are not succeeding is due to your professor, I can guarantee you that telling your professor this will not be to your benefit. Realize that professors are human and can make mistakes and they often do. The professor is not trying to make your life more miserable and most will attempt to rectify their mistakes, if brought to their attention.

However, when students write emails in disrespectful ways and blame them for mistakes or for the student's lack of success, this puts anyone on the defensive which may end up putting more stress on you. Instead, if you believe a professor has made a mistake, then you should email them asking for clarification.

When you need help in your class, you should reach out to peers and your professor. It is essential to know what is important and how to successfully reach out to your professor. Monitoring the timing and the frequency of your contacts with your professor is essential to receiving the needed information. Remember to be respectful to your professor, especially in email, and have well-structured and detailed emails when you do contact them.

Ultimately, please realize that being responsible for your learning does not mean being completely independent; instead, it means knowing when, why, and how to appropriately reach out and to whom.

CONCLUSION

Throughout this book, my goal was focused on allowing others to learn and benefit from my experiences to start being a responsible student earlier in their academic careers. While there have been several up and downs in my life as a student, I can say that learning to change my perceptions and developing the skills that allowed me to focus my work better has greatly changed my ability to perform as a student and in my career.

In fact, often when I describe what I have accomplished in my schoolwork, many people have asked me how it is even possible that I have accomplished that mycg work in the time frame. While my own talents may increase my ability to perform as a student, specific skills that I have discussed in this book were required for me to be successful.

After college, I went to graduate school to obtain my Ph.D. in chemistry with a minor in women's and gender studies. A typical Ph.D. program takes about 5-7 years and I was told with adding a minor that I should expect for it to take even longer. For a science Ph.D., your degree is dependent more on the accomplishment of research than on coursework. Therefore, with the capabilities to focus on work, understanding what I need to do to be successful, and altering my perception on how to be my best student, I finished my Ph.D. with a minor in 3 1/2 years. When people hear this, they often believe that I never sleep or have no social life. But in fact, I regularly went out with friends and slept plenty throughout graduate school.

Throughout my entire academic career, I have never resembled a perfect student, especially my version of perfect. I was never the student in the library studying all the time, getting up early to start getting work done, or even making sure I att class early. On the other hand, I am a successful student in my own unique way without a routine using motivation for my goals and allowing myself to be the type of student that works the best for me.

Throughout graduate school, there were only a few times that I found myself being overly stressed out. Instead, I was excited to do most of the work that I did. I saw my coursework assignments as opportunities that allowed me to explore areas of interest or push forward my research. I understood how to get the most benefit from the least effort and do it ethically. Instead of failing to get the correct information or becoming overwhelmed with frustration, I knew when it was best to reach out to my fellow colleagues or professors to continue to be productive.

I hope that through this book, you have been motivated to consider a change to your perspective on what a responsible student looks and acts like. My goal is that you can now see how you can fit the mode of a responsible student and feel better equipped with skills to be able to handle the different challenges and frustrations you may experience in your academic career.

One of my favorite quotes is by Randy Pausch:

> *"The brick walls are there for a reason. The brick walls are not there to keep us out. The brick walls are there to give us a chance to show how badly we want something."*

In some cases, to go through the brick walls you must learn the skills of scaling or deconstructing the wall, whichever the requirement calls for. My goal in this book is to give you the skills to be successful in your schooling. However, to fulfill the success in your studies you must want it badly enough to practice these skills into strong habits.

I wish you all the best with your future studies.

Made in the USA
Columbia, SC
09 January 2025